Snow V

by Sheree

Contents

Act 1	Scene 1	3	Act 2	Scene 1	13
	Scene 2	5		Scene 2	18
	Scene 3	7		Scene 3	20
	Scene 4	9		Scene 4	21
	Scene 5	11		Scene 5	23

Cast List

Narrator

Interrupter

Evil Queen

Magic Mirror

Snow White

Woodsman

Combat Boots Snow White

Pedlar Woman

Journalist

7 Dwarves:

   Stinky

   Lazy

   Crazy

   Nerdy

   Naughty

   Tidy

   Fred

Forest Nasty 1

Forest Nasty 2

Forest Nasty 3

The Woods

Act 1
Scene 1

Narrator:	Once upon a time …
Interrupter:	Hang on. Wait there. Hold it a minute.
Narrator:	What?
Interrupter:	*(Copying Narrator)* 'Once upon a time …' Surely you can come up with something a bit more original than 'Once upon a time'?
Narrator:	It's a fairytale.
Interrupter:	So?
Narrator:	It *always* starts with 'Once upon a time …'
Interrupter:	Why?
Narrator:	Because it does!
Interrupter:	Why can't it start with 'Away in the dark-flung corners of the world …' or 'Yo! Listen to this'?
Narrator:	*(Ignoring Interrupter)* Once upon a time …
Interrupter:	In a galaxy far, far away …
Narrator:	Shoosh.
Interrupter:	I'm just trying to liven things up a bit.
Narrator:	Things don't need 'livening up a bit'.
Interrupter:	Yes they do.
Narrator:	Can I get on with the story?
Interrupter:	*(Pause)* Yes.
Narrator:	Thank you. Once upon a time …

Interrupter:	*(Shouting)* The goblins are coming. The goblins are coming.
Narrator:	*(Angry)* Stop it!
Interrupter:	Sorry.
Narrator:	… there was a Queen whose only wish was to have a baby daughter. She would sit, year after year, season after season, just praying for her wish to come true. One winter, while she was sewing by the window, she pricked her finger and the red blood fell on the white snow.
Interrupter:	Ooops. Clumsy.
Narrator:	Looking at the red blood on the white snow, she repeated her wish for a daughter, whose skin would be as white as snow and whose lips as red as blood. A year later, her daughter was born.

Interrupter:	Hang on a minute.
Narrator:	What now?
Interrupter:	So she pricked her finger, saw the colours and had a baby based on those colours?
Narrator:	Yes.
Interrupter:	Well, it's a good thing she wasn't eating bangers and mash at the time. She'd have ended up with a sausage and potato-coloured baby. Yuk.

Narrator:	*(Turning back to the audience)* Finally her wish was granted, but within a year of Snow White being born, the Queen died.
Interrupter:	Oh, how sad.
Narrator:	The King, lonely without his wife, remarried.
Interrupter:	Don't tell me, I bet she's evil.
Narrator:	Evil, wicked and vain – looking every day into her Magic Mirror.
Interrupter:	Mirror, Mirror, here I stand. Who's the fairest in the land?
Narrator:	And so our story begins. Snow White is now sixteen, the Evil Queen is continually mean and as for the King …
Interrupter:	He looks like a string bean!
Narrator:	So I take you now to the castle high, Where the Evil Queen is standing by. And in her clutches Snow White fair, Will soon come into great despair.
Interrupter:	Why are you speaking in rhyme?
Narrator:	I have no idea.

They both exit.

Scene 2

The castle. Evil Queen enters with Magic Mirror.
Evil Queen is extremely posh and vain.

Evil Queen:	Mirror, Mirror, here I stand. Who's the fairest in the land?
Magic Mirror:	Guess.
Evil Queen:	Me?

5

Magic Mirror: No. Guess again.

Evil Queen: Me!

Magic Mirror: No. Guess again.

Evil Queen: WHAT!!!???

Magic Mirror: Look Queenie, your looks are going and you're getting older. It happens to everyone.

Evil Queen: But I've got an excellent plastic surgeon.

Magic Mirror: It doesn't matter. You're over-the-hill, past your prime, OLD!

Evil Queen: I am not old!

Magic Mirror: You're older than Snow White.

Evil Queen: Snow White! Is that who's prettier than me?

Magic Mirror: Might be.

Evil Queen: Well, we'll soon see about that. *(Pulls out her mobile phone)* Yes hello, this is the palace calling. Do you have a spare woodsman? You do? Great! I need someone who's good with an axe. Thank you. Goodbye.

Magic Mirror: Planning on chopping off Snow White's head, huh?

Evil Queen: Might be.

Scene 3

Snow White enters with birthday cake.

Snow White: *(Excited. Singing to herself. Behaving like a spoilt child)* Happy birthday to me, happy birthday to me. Happy birthday, Snow White. Happy birthday to me.

Blows out the candles.

(To Evil Queen) Did you get me a birthday present? Huh? Huh? Did you? Did you?

Evil Queen: Yes dear, but it's hidden in the woods.

Snow White: What did you put it there for? That's a bit silly. I don't want a present that's all covered in mud.

Evil Queen: But it's a special birthday present.

Snow White: That's what you said last year when you gave me that man-eating plant, and the year before, when you gave me a guillotine.

Evil Queen: It's better than both of those put together.

Snow White: I hope so.

Narrator enters and the action on stage freezes.

Narrator: Hang on a minute. That's not how I remember Snow White. She wasn't some spoilt brat. She was lovely and sweet and caring.

Interrupter: And boring.

Narrator: *(Angry)* Will you stop changing the story. Let's go back to Snow White's entrance …

Narrator and Interrupter exit as the characters rewind to the start scene again.

Snow White:	*(Excited. Singing to herself. Very sweet this time.)* Happy birthday to me, happy birthday to me. Happy birthday, Snow White. Happy birthday to me.

Blows out the candles.

Evil Queen:	*(Sarcastic)* Snow White dear, I hear one of your little forest creatures is very sick.
Snow White:	Oh no. Which one?
Evil Queen:	*(Angry)* I don't know which one. *(Suddenly changing)* Oh, actually I think it was one of the little fluffy bunny rabbits.
Snow White:	Then I must go to the woods and nurse it back to health.
Evil Queen:	Well, if you think you must.
Snow White:	Oh yes. The little, fluffy bunny rabbit could be dying.
Evil Queen:	Be careful and don't be gone too long.
Snow White:	I won't, Evil Stepmother. It's so nice of you to care.

Snow White exits.

Evil Queen:	Urgh! How nauseating. Now, where's that woodsman?

Woodsman enters. Very dumb and docile. Stands staring, until the Evil Queen notices him.

Evil Queen:	Are you the woodsman?
Woodsman:	Uh huh.
Evil Queen:	Do you have an axe?
Woodsman:	Uh huh.
Evil Queen:	Is it sharp?

Woodsman: Uh huh.

Evil Queen: Good. I want you to go out into the woods. Find Snow White. Chop off her head and bring me back her heart. Do you understand?

Woodsman: Uh huh.

Pause. Woodsman doesn't move and continues to stand and stare, mouth open.

Evil Queen: Well then ... Go! *(Pause)* Now!

Woodsman: Uh huh.

Woodsman exits.

Evil Queen: You just can't get the help these days.

Evil Queen exits with Magic Mirror.

Scene 4

The woods. The Woods enter and take up their position on stage. **Note:** *The Forest Nasties can be hiding amongst the woods. Snow White enters, followed closely by the Woodsman.*

Snow White: *(Calling)* Here, bunny bunny.

Snow White turns around and the Woodsman freezes so as not to be noticed. This creeping and freezing routine continues for a short time until Snow White eventually catches him.

Snow White: *(Light and joking)* Are you following me?

Woodsman: Uh huh.

Snow White: *(Sees axe)* Have you been sent to kill me?

Woodsman: Uh huh.

Snow White: Well why didn't you say so? Who sent you? Was it my Evil Stepmother?

Woodsman: Uh huh.

Snow White: Thought so. I had a feeling she didn't like me very much.

The Woodsman lifts his axe and walks slowly towards her.

Snow White: *(Getting scared)* Now wait a minute. If you kill me, it'll be murder and you'll go to prison for a very long time.

Woodsman: Uh huh.

Snow White: How about we make a deal?

The Woodsman stops, axe still in the air and listens to her deal.

Snow White: I'll run away into the woods and *pretend* to be dead ...

Woodsman: Uh huh.

Snow White: ... and you can kill something else and *pretend* it's me ...

Woodsman: Uh huh.

Snow White: ... and the Evil Queen can go on *pretending* to be the prettiest in the land!

Woodsman: Uh huh.

Snow White: Besides, *you* don't have to kill me. Hunger, cold and the fear of Forest Nasties probably will.

Woodsman: Uh huh.

Pause.

Snow White: Do we have a deal?

Pause.

Woodsman: Uh huh.

Woodsman puts his axe down.

Snow White: *(Breathing a sigh of relief)* Phew! *(Joking again)* Thought I was a goner for a minute there.

Woodsman: Uh huh.

She makes to leave.

Snow White: Will you be alright finding your way back to the castle in the dark?

Woodsman: Uh huh.

Snow White: Well, I'd better go away and pretend to be dead somewhere.

Woodsman: Uh huh.

Snow White: Bye.

Snow White exits.

Scene 5

Woodsman just stands there for a while until the Journalist enters.

Journalist: And here we are, live at the spot where Snow White was last seen. We have an actual eye-witness to her disappearance – Mr Woodsman. You are a woodsman, are you not?

Woodsman: Uh huh.

Journalist: And it was on this very spot that you last saw Snow White, looking for a sick bunny rabbit?

Woodsman: Uh huh.

Journalist: And what was the last thing you said to her?

Woodsman: Uh huh.

Journalist: Thank you, Mr Woodsman. *(Woodsman exits.)* That's right, everybody. Snow White is missing, presumed dead. Now for the rest of today's top stories ... Break-in at the Bears' house deemed a hoax. Goldilocks demands justice. Enquiry begins today. Rapunzel gets a haircut and Rumpelstiltskin states 'I'm changing my name'. This is Fairytale News, signing off.

Journalist exits and, as he does, Snow White enters and bumps into him.

Journalist: Watch where you're going.

Snow White: Sorry.

Forest Nasties jump out.

Forest Nasty 1: Boo!

Snow White: *(Jumps in fright)* Oh you scared me. Are you a Forest Nasty?

Forest Nasty 1: Yes.

Forest Nasty 2: Boo!

Snow White: Oh! You too?

Forest Nasty 2: Yes.

Forest Nasty 3: And me! Boo!

Snow White: Oh ... Help!

Snow White gets chased by the Forest Nasties.
Note: *This chase is not confined to the stage. Eventually Snow White makes her way through the woods to the Dwarves' cottage.*

Snow White: *(To Forest Nasties who are unable to enter Dwarves' Cottage.)* Ha, ha! You didn't get me.

Forest Nasties sulk off disappointed, followed by the Woods.

Snow White: *(Entering the cottage)* Phew! That was close.

Act 2

Scene 1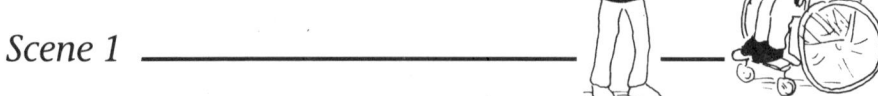

The Dwarves' cottage. Snow White lies asleep in the corner. The Dwarves enter one by one and take up their place around the table, not realising Snow White is there.

Fred: Oh Yuk! Naughty pushed Stinky in the mud pile again.

Naughty: I did not. He tripped and fell.

Stinky enters all grubby and sits beside Lazy.

Lazy: Phwoah! Stinky, you smell.

Stinky: I fell in the mud again.

Tidy: Will someone clean him up?

Lazy: I'm not cleaning him up.

Fred: You never clean anything up.

Nerdy: Naughty, what have you done with my glasses?

Naughty: Nothing.

Nerdy: I can't see anything without my glasses. Phwoah! What's that smell?

All Dwarves: Stinky!

Stinky: I fell in the mud again.

Tidy: Lazy, go find Nerdy's glasses.

Lazy: No.

Lazy puts his feet on the table ready for a nap.

Tidy: And get your feet off the table.

Lazy yawns and falls asleep.

13

Nerdy:	*(To Fred)* Tidy, I can't see anything without my glasses.
Fred:	I'm Fred. That's Tidy.
Nerdy:	Tidy, I can't see anything without my glasses.
Naughty:	Are these your glasses, Nerdy?

Gives him a huge pair of odd-looking sunglasses. Nerdy puts them on and all the Dwarves laugh.

Nerdy:	No, this isn't them.
Naughty:	Well, what about these?

Gives him another pair, just as silly.

Nerdy:	No.
Tidy:	Naughty, give Nerdy back his glasses.
Naughty:	I don't have them. Crazy took them.
Fred:	Where is Crazy anyway?

Just then Crazy enters wearing Nerdy's glasses and bounds around the room like a cartoon character.

Crazy:	Yip, yip, yop, yop. I think I'm a balloon animal.
Fred:	There he is.
Tidy:	Get him, boys.

Everyone but Lazy gets up and puts Crazy into a straitjacket. Confusion and cries of Help! from Crazy. Once Crazy is in the straitjacket they all go back to their seats and sit down. Crazy then stands, arms in straitjacket and suddenly sounds quite normal.

Crazy:	Hello everyone. What's for dinner?
Fred:	Nothing.
Naughty:	Lazy didn't cook.
Crazy:	What's that smell?
All Dwarves:	Stinky!
Stinky:	I fell in the mud again.
Nerdy:	Have you got my glasses, Crazy?
Crazy:	Yes, here they are. I was using them to contact my friends on Jupiter.
Nerdy:	Thanks.

Nerdy puts on his glasses and while everyone else is still talking he notices Snow White and slowly creeps up to her.

Fred:	Well I'm hungry.
Crazy:	Me too.
Naughty:	I think we should eat Lazy.
Lazy:	I heard that.
Tidy:	Well, we've got to eat something.
Nerdy:	Hey guys. I think I've found something.
Fred:	Great.
Stinky:	Can we eat it?
Nerdy:	Come and have a look.

All the Dwarves go over to where Snow White is lying.

15

Fred:	Somebody'd better wake her up.
Tidy:	She's making the place untidy.
Naughty:	I've got an idea. Everyone stand back.

They all stand back and he pushes Stinky forward. Snow White, eyes closed, starts sniffing the air. She suddenly sits bolt upright and looks at the Dwarves.

Snow White:	Oh my. What's that smell?
All Dwarves:	Stinky.
Stinky:	I fell in the mud again.
Fred:	And who are you?
Snow White:	I'm Snow White.
All Dwarves:	Snow White!
Snow White:	Yes.
Nerdy:	Who's that?
Tidy:	You know, the Evil Queen's daughter.
Snow White:	Step-daughter.
Fred:	Aren't you supposed to be dead?
Snow White:	Yes.
Crazy:	Does that mean we can eat her?
All Dwarves:	No!
Snow White:	Everyone just *thinks* I'm dead.
Lazy:	That's a good plan. You don't have to do any work if you're dead.
Snow White:	I can't go back to the castle.
Naughty:	Why not? Did you do something naughty?
Snow White:	No. The Evil Queen hates me.

Fred:	You could stay here.
All Dwarves:	Yes!
Snow White:	Oh, that would be lovely.
Fred:	Can you cook?
Tidy:	Can you clean?
Crazy:	Have you ever communicated with the little green men on Mars and taken a bite out of the moon?
Snow White:	What?
Tidy:	I think we need to have a meeting. All those in favour say Aye!
All Dwarves:	Aye!
Fred:	All those against say Aye!
All Dwarves:	Aye!
Nerdy:	Alright. You can stay.
Tidy:	But only if you clean.
Fred:	And cook.
Stinky:	And wash my clothes.
Snow White:	Well, I think I can do that.

Dwarves and Snow White freeze.

Scene 2

Interrupter and Narrator enter.

Interrupter: Wait, wait, wait! Clean our house, cook our dinner and wash our clothes and you can stay?

Narrator: Yes.

Interrupter: That's not what Snow White should do.

Narrator: No? And what do you think she should do?

Interrupter: I'll show you. *(He blows a whistle)*

Enter Combat Boots Snow White. She pushes the other Snow White out of the way and proceeds to give the 7 Dwarves battle instructions.

Combat Boots: *(Leaning over the table as if examining battle plans)* Right, Stinky, you go around and create a diversion at the back of the castle. Tidy and Fred will use Crazy as a catapult to break into the top window of the tower. Naughty, you and Lazy set up the booby traps in the castle moat and remember, everyone, this mission is of the highest importance.

Fred: What about the Evil Queen?

Combat Boots: Leave her to me. I'll dispose of her myself. This time – it's personal.

Nerdy: What do you want me to do?

Combat Boots: Nerdy, you're in charge of communications. Any enemy messages must be scrambled and their Internet access denied. Got it?

Nerdy: Yep!

Combat Boots: Is everyone ready?

All Dwarves: Yep!

Combat Boots: Is everyone with me?

All Dwarves: Yep!

Combat Boots: OK! Let's storm the castle …

All exit with excited war cries.

All: Charge …

Leaving Narrator, Interrupter and the real Snow White on stage alone.

Narrator:	Yes, well, in some parallel universe *maybe* that would happen, but getting back to the story, the *real* Snow White cooked and cleaned and washed ...
Interrupter:	*(Disappointed)* You mean she didn't storm the castle?
Narrator:	No. She cooked and cleaned ...
	The real Snow White starts cleaning up the Dwarves' cottage on stage.
Narrator:	... unaware that the Evil Queen was still plotting her death.
Interrupter:	So she did all that work for nothing? Typical.

Everyone exits.

Scene 3

The castle. Evil Queen and Magic Mirror enter.

Evil Queen:	Mirror, Mirror, here I stand. Who's the fairest in the land?
Magic Mirror:	Alright Queenie, with all my might. It isn't you, it's still Snow White.
Evil Queen:	It can't be Snow White. I killed her. Didn't I?
Magic Mirror:	No.
Evil Queen:	Oh this is really starting to annoy me. She's supposed to be dead.
Magic Mirror:	I told you that Woodsman was no good.
Evil Queen:	Well. If at first you don't succeed ...
Magic Mirror:	Give up?
Evil Queen:	No! Try and try again!
Magic Mirror:	What are you going to do now, my old queen?

Evil Queen: I am not old! I'm going to find Snow White and kill her myself.

Magic Mirror: Don't you think she'll suspect something?

Evil Queen: Not if I'm in disguise ...

Evil Queen disappears behind the dressing screen. Various items of clothing get thrown over.

Evil Queen: *(From behind the screen)* Oh I never have a thing to wear ...

Pedlar Woman comes out from behind screen.

Pedlar Woman: How do I look?

Magic Mirror: You look like a completely different person.

Pedlar Woman: Good. Now to tempt Snow White.

She goes off laughing, followed by the Magic Mirror.

Scene 4

The woods . The Woods and Forest Nasties re-enter and take up their positions as before.

Pedlar Woman: *(Chanting)* Ribbons and bows. Ribbons and bows. To do your pretty hair ...

All 3 Nasties: *(To Pedlar Woman)* Boo!

Pedlar Woman: Get out of my way.

21

Forest Nasties, disappointed and upset, sulk off the stage followed by the Woods. Pedlar Woman arrives at the Dwarves' house.

Pedlar Woman: *(Chanting)* Ribbons and bows. Ribbons and bows. To do your pretty hair. Ribbons and bows. Ribbons and bows. For those who look so fair.

Snow White: Oh how lovely. I haven't been shopping for ages.

Pedlar Woman: Come try. Come try. *(Pedlar Woman holds up a selection of ribbons.)*

Snow White: The red or the blue? Hmm. I can't decide.

Pedlar Woman: Why not have both, sweet child?

Snow White: *(Haggling. Very quick pace)* How much?

Pedlar Woman: Six pence.

Snow White: Four.

Pedlar Woman: Five.

Snow White: Sold! What else do you have?

Pedlar Woman: Brushes and combs. Brushes and combs. To do your pretty hair. Brushes and combs. Brushes and combs. For those who look so fair.

Interrupter: Hold it. Wait there a moment. *(The on-stage action freezes again)* I'm sorry, but how stupid is Snow White? *(Mimicking her)* 'Oh gee, the Evil Queen is after me, so what do I do? Open the door to strangers.' And another thing. Why doesn't the peasant woman bring something useful, like a washing machine or microwave oven? I mean, if Snow White *has* to earn her keep by cooking and cleaning she should at least have all the mod cons.

Narrator: Will you stop interrupting. *(Ushering him off the stage)* Let them tell the story.

The action continues.

Pedlar Woman: I have a beautiful comb here.
Snow White: How much?
Pedlar Woman: Six pence.
Snow White: Four.
Pedlar Woman: Five.
Snow White: Sold!
Pedlar Woman: And now, for helping out a poor, defenceless old woman, let me give you this nice big juicy apple for free.
Snow White: Oh thank you. How lovely.
Pedlar Woman: That's right. Just take a nice big bite.

Snow White bites into the apple and drops down dead. The Pedlar Woman exits, laughing. There is a pause ...

Scene 5

Interrupter: What? Is that it? She's dead?
Narrator: Well what did you expect?
Interrupter: She can't die.
Narrator: I thought that's what you wanted.
Interrupter: Yeah, but what about 'happily ever after'?
Narrator: Doesn't happen.
Interrupter: It's a fairytale. It's supposed to end with 'happily ever after'.
Narrator: Not this time. *(Turning to the audience)* The Evil Queen went back to being the fairest in the land and Snow White, too beautiful to bury in the ground, was displayed in a glass coffin and guarded by the Seven Dwarves day and night.

Interrupter: They put a dead body on display – yuk!

Narrator: Life continued at the castle until …

Combat Boots Snow White enters with the 7 Dwarves.

Combat Boots: Right Stinky, revive her!

Stinky steps forward and waves his armpits in Snow White's general direction. She sniffs the air a couple of times before sitting bolt upright!

Snow White: Phoah! What's that smell?

All Dwarves: Stinky!

Stinky: I knew my smell would come in handy one day.

Combat Boots: Right! Everyone to the castle. We've got a Queen to kill.

All exit with excited war cries.

All: Charge …

Snow White: Hang on. Wait for me.

Snow White exits, chasing after them. Narrator and Interrupter are left on stage.

Interrupter: You tricked me.

Narrator: Yep!

Interrupter: Did they kill the Queen?

Narrator: Yep!

Interrupter: And did everyone live 'happily ever after'?

Narrator: Yep!

Interrupter: Good.

THE END